DK 24 HOURS
Rain Forest

DK

LONDON, NEW YORK, MUNICH,
MELBOURNE, and DELHI

Written and edited by Fleur Star
Designed by Jacqueline Gooden

DTP designer Almudena Díaz
Picture researcher Jo Walton
Production Lucy Baker
Jacket copywriter Adam Powley

Publishing manager Susan Leonard

Consultants Kerstin Swahn,
Julio Bernal, and Evan Bowen-Jones
of Fauna & Flora International

With thanks to Lisa Magloff for
project development

First American Edition, 2006

Published in the United States by
DK Publishing, Inc., 375 Hudson Street,
New York, NY 10014

06 07 08 09 10   10 9 8 7 6 5 4 3 2 1

A Cataloging-in-Publication record for this book
is available from the Library of Congress.

ISBN-13: 978-0-7566-1985-5
ISBN-10: 0-7566-1985-8

DK books are available at special discounts for bulk
purchases for sales promotions, premiums, fund-raising, or
educational use. For details, contact: DK Publishing Special
Markets, 375 Hudson Street, New York, NY 10014
or SpecialSales@dk.com

Color reproduction by Colourscan, Singapore
Printed and bound in China
by L. Rex Printing Co. Ltd.

Discover more at
www.dk.com

Welcome to the Amazon

6:00 am Dawn

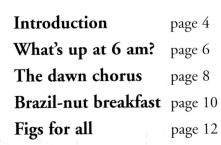

10:00 am Morning

The rain forest is as busy as a city, and the creatures that live there behave much like us. Spend **24 hours** with some of its colorful characters and discover how they eat, sleep, rest, and play.

rain forest, the biggest jungle in the world.

2:00 pm Afternoon

6:00 pm Dusk

10:00 pm Night

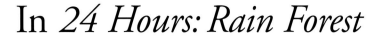
In *24 Hours: Rain Forest*

we spend a day and night in the Amazon rain forest to look at the creatures that live there. During the 24 hours, we return to the four animals and one plant shown on this page to see what they are doing.

Capuchin monkey

One of the smaller monkey species, the 14-in- (35-cm-) tall capuchins have tails as long as their bodies. The tail is useful for hanging off branches or as a fifth limb when walking on "all fours." Capuchins also walk upright to carry food.

Jaguar

Jaguars are solitary animals, living alone except for mothers raising their cubs. They are the biggest cats in the Americas, and can grow up to 6 ft (1.8 m) from head to tail.

The world's biggest rain forest, the Amazon, covers two-fifths of South America. The Amazon River snakes through it.

Scale Look for scale guides as you read through the book. They will help you to figure out the size of the creatures you meet. The children are 3 ft 9 in (115 cm) tall, and the hand is 5½ in (14 cm) from fingertip to wrist.

Seasons in the rain forest

8:02 am This book shows the rain forest in the dry season. In the wet season, March to August, it can get flooded. Time boxes show how quickly things change in the forest.

Scarlet macaw

There are no prizes for guessing how the scarlet macaw got its name! Often seen flying in pairs, the bird reaches speeds of 35 mph (55 km/h). It measures 35 in (90 cm) from head to tail.

Heliconia

Heliconia plants are also known as "lobster claws" or "parrots' bills" because of the shape of their bracts—the bright red leaves that surround the plant's flowers.

Blue morpho butterfly

The colorful wings of a blue morpho butterfly measure between 5 and 8 in (12 and 20 cm) wide. The male is brighter blue so he can attract females.

An emergent tree breaks through the rain-forest canopy.

Dawn is a swift affair in the Amazon, so close to the equator. Sunrise is at the same time all year. As soon as the sun climbs above the canopy, it begins to filter through the trees to warm the forest.

The **jaguar** is settling down to sleep after a successful night's hunting. On lean days, jaguars will continue to hunt through the day.

The **capuchin monkey** is just beginning its day. It moves from its sleeping tree to an eating tree, where it peels the bark, looking for insects.

Scarlet macaws flock together at the clay lick before breakfast. Eating clay protects them against getting ill from the toxins in the seeds they eat.

The **blue morpho** is pupating—changing from a caterpillar to a butterfly. Its chrysalis has been hanging off of a leaf for a few weeks now.

Hummingbirds are ideal pollinators of **heliconia** flowers. Attracted by the plant's bright red bracts, the birds are rewarded with plenty of nectar.

Howler monkeys are noisy beasts! Having woken the rain forest at dawn with their loud roars, which can be heard 10 miles (16 km) away, they go foraging for breakfast.

Howlers can hang upside-down to feast on fruit and leaves.

Howler monkeys do not like chance meetings, which could lead to fighting over food. So they call out to tell each other where they are.

A baby hangs on to its mother's fur. It is too young to forage for itself.

Both red howler and black howler species live in the Amazon rain forest. . . . .

Howwwll

Call of nature

The dawn chorus starts with a single male howler's call, which sounds like a breathless bark. Other howlers join in, and the howls grow louder and longer until a roar fills the forest.

Once the macaws

have lined their stomachs with clay, they may fly to a Brazil nut tree for a nutty breakfast. Howler monkeys, sloths, and caterpillars can also be found in the tree's canopy, munching on the juicy green leaves.

No animal could eat Brazil nuts if it weren't for the **agouti**. It is the only creature that can break through the tough outer pod, releasing the nuts inside.

Living for up to 1,000 years, Brazil-nut trees are the oldest in the forest. They are also among the tallest, and can even change the local weather! Together they release enough water from their leaves to form rain clouds.

"I'll **nibble** a few nuts now, and bury the rest for later."

The agouti chisels through the pod with its sharp rodent teeth.

Brazil nuts are clustered inside a pod as heavy as a cannonball.

Capuchins drink the nuts' oil as well as eating the kernels.

Bright blue bees are the key to the Brazil nut's success. They are the only insect that can pollinate the tree—and if there is no pollination, there are no seeds and no new trees.

These bees are called orchid bees because they use the scent of orchids to attract mates.

A buzz of activity surrounds a fig tree,

with many different animals turning up to feed on figs. The trees produce fruit all year, even during the dry season when other trees are bare.

The cycle of life

9:15 am Figs can only be pollinated by tiny fig wasps. The female crawls inside through a tiny hole, carrying pollen with her.

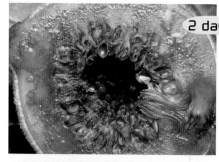

2 days later She lays her eggs inside the fig, pollinating the flowers at the same time. Fig wasps can only reproduce inside figs.

Up to 20 species of fig trees can grow together in the same area of forest, each with its own shape and size of fruit. The largest is the size of a tennis ball.

30 days later The young wasps leave home and fly to another fig to lay their own eggs, taking pollen with them, and the cycle begins again.

A fig is made up of lots of flowers growing inside a skin...

Figs can only ripen if they have been pollinated. The wasps leave the fruit before it ripens.

12

Vines and lianas grow on most trees in the rain forest, weighing them down and competing for light and nutrients. Trees try to get rid of the vines by swaying or even dropping branches.

Large buttress roots are a sign that the rain-forest soil is shallow. They grow above the ground to keep the tree stable..

More animals eat figs than any other fruit...

Butterflies feast on figs on the forest floor. A butterfly cannot chew; instead, it sucks up fruit pulp through its tube-shaped mouth, called a proboscis.

Safe in its roost, a **tent-making bat** eats a fig fresh from the tree. It carefully peels away the unripe skin with its teeth before eating the seeds inside.

A **coati-mundi** uses its long snout for sniffing out food, but it doesn't need to work hard at foraging when there are easy pickings in the tree.

The strong bill of a **blue and yellow macaw** rips through fig skin easily. Macaws are the only birds that can pick up food in their claws to bring it to their mouths.

1 Jaguar   2 Spider monkey

Midmorning, the

sun streams through the trees and heats the forest to 80°F (27°C). An alert jaguar finds a shady spot on the forest floor. It would usually be asleep during the day, but hunger drives it to hunt.

14

Up in a tree, the **jaguar's** spotted fur looks like sunlight shining through the leaves. It has no tree-climbing predators and can sleep safely up there.

Apart from a nap at noon, **capuchins** spend much of the day eating. They are very intelligent and use tools such as stones to crack nutshells.

A **macaw's** strong bill is not just a mouth, it is an extra limb. As well as crushing food, the macaw's bill can grip branches while climbing.

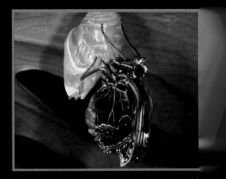

The **blue morpho** chrysalis splits and, after 20 minutes, the imago—adult butterfly—emerges. It then rests for two hours to dry its wings.

Tent-making bats use large **heliconia** leaves as a daytime roost. They chew the leaves to make them droop, giving shelter from rain, sun, and predators.

A smash-and-grab raid is taking place in broad daylight. A giant anteater has sniffed out a termite mound, and sits down to dig its snout into a meal. Its long, thin tongue dips in and out of the nest 160 times a minute, scooping up the insects.

Anteaters' long snouts are not just straws for sucking up food; they also use their noses to find ants' nests and termite mounds. They have poor eyesight, so they rely on their sense of smell. If the insects are hard to reach, anteaters will rip the nests apart with their powerful claws.

Azteca ants fight back

11:00 am Azteca ants, a favorite of tamandua anteaters, live inside cecropia tree branches. The tree even provides food for the ants.

1 day later Without damaging the tree, the queen ant lays her eggs inside a narrow stem. It is a home safe from predators.

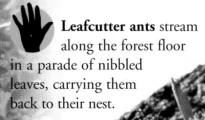

8 days later In return, the ants attack animals that eat the tree. They can also see off tamanduas with a flurry of bites.

Leafcutter ants stream along the forest floor in a parade of nibbled leaves, carrying them back to their nest.

The ants feed on fungus, which grows on the chewed leaves.

17

Every rain forest around the world is home to primates, from Asian orangutans to Madagascan lemurs. South America seems to specialize in small monkeys that enjoy playing in the sun!

Tree-dwelling tamarins eat whatever they can find in the canopy, from eggs to fruit.

Spider monkeys have small or no thumbs on their hands: swinging through trees is easier with just four fingers.

Squirrel-sized **tamarins** get around by leaping between trees. They can jump 65 ft (20 m) to the ground and land unhurt.

All **silvery marmosets** are born as twins. They feed on sap straight from the tree.

Spider monkeys are the rain-forest acrobats, active all day and using their tails for climbing. But they do not climb too high in the canopy, to avoid becoming a harpy eagle's lunch.

Only younger **woolly monkeys** have enough energy to be active at noon. Their parents are resting. Like many larger primates, they prefer a leisurely meal or grooming session to playing.

A **squirrel monkey** pauses in its constant search for fruit to deal with one of the drawbacks of being a furry animal: fleas.

The tail is flexible and sensitive enough to pick up food.

Bald uakaris have long, red fur everywhere except on their faces. They choose their mates by the color of their face: the redder the head, the healthier and more attractive it is to potential partners.

The smallest monkey in the world, a **pygmy marmoset** is tiny enough to hide among leaves in the canopy.

19

A wingspan of 7 ft (2 m) makes this the world's largest eagle.

Each talon is as long as a finger. At 3 in (7 cm) long, the hind talon does the most damage.

It's time for lunch, and a harpy eagle—one of the world's most powerful birds—leaves its chick to hunt for food.

The eagle has landed

At last the mother returns to the nest with what's left of the kill, and the chick gets fed. It will not rely on her for long: by the age of ten months, it can hunt for itself.

Watching and waiting

A young chick keeps an eye out for its mother to return from the hunt. Harpy eagles hunt in the canopy, swooping down on a variety of prey, from sloths to snakes.

Small mammals are no problem for a **bill and claws.**

The hooked bill is a vicious tool for ripping into prey.

21

1 Red-eyed tree frog

A n unexpected heavy rain shower has started. It lasts a brief 30 minutes—but sometimes it rains for days. The rain disrupts life in the canopy, waking a nocturnal frog, which seems happy to take a warm shower.

The **jaguar** has found shelter in dense brush to avoid the rain. A short shower barely reaches the forest floor through the closely growing trees.

The sociable **capuchins** have stopped their daytime grooming and foraging to shelter from the rain. They huddle together for warmth.

Macaws should be out finding food for their chicks, but the rain forces them to stay in their nest. Many chicks starve during heavy rains.

Having dried its wings, which are now bright and shimmering, the **blue morpho** flies down to the forest floor to eat its first meal as an adult.

Rainwater collects in the **heliconia's** bracts, where insects such as mosquitoes lay their eggs. Bigger animals will also drink the water.

The rain has stopped, the heat returns, and the animals reappear. Or do they? Some of them are hard to spot. Insects use camouflage to hide from predators, but iguanas blend in with trees so they can catch insects undetected.

Iguanas also stay hidden to avoid predators. If spotted, they will drop off the branches to escape being caught. Iguanas can fall more than 60 ft (18 m) without being hurt.

The fixed pose of a **praying mantis** can easily be mistaken for a twig.

Some insects have weird disguises to stay hidden in the daytime.

The underside of a **blue morpho's** wings is not blue, but brown— the perfect camouflage for the forest floor.

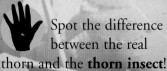

Spot the difference between the real thorn and the **thorn insect!**

24

Katydids are masters of disguise. A **dead-leaf katydid** becomes part of the forest floor…

Is this an owl or an **owl butterfly**? The insect has "eye spots" on its wings to confuse and scare off predators such as pacas, which are targets for owls.

…while up in the tree, a **green-leaf katydid** is just one of the crowd.

Lichen grows on some tree trunks. It is a safe home for the spiky **lichen katydid**.

Eek!

…A **conehead katydid's** spines are used for defense, but they also help the insect hide among thorns.

Far from hiding in the understory

like insects, birds are a noticeable part of the rain forest. Males are free to show off their bright colors to attract females; at the first sign of a predator, they quickly fly away.

A **toucan** reaches out with its bill to pluck fruit. Its bill is so long, it has to toss its head back and throw the fig into its throat to swallow it.

The **cock of the rock** lives in mountainous parts of the forest. It is vital to the forests because it disperses the seeds of many trees.

The **scarlet tanager** is one of the few rain-forest birds that migrates, spending the summer in North America.

Watch the birdie

The manakin's courtship dance includes raising its tail and cracking it like a whip.

Two male **manakins** put on a display in their lek, an area where birds show off to attract mates.

Of the 27 species of parrots in the rain forest, the **hyacinth macaw** stands head and shoulders above the rest, being 3 ft (1 m) long from head to tail. These macaws are usually seen in the trees, only coming to the ground for food.

Many tank bromeliads grow on trees, using them to get near the sunlight. Other bromeliads live on the ground.

Bromeliads are ideal daytime hideouts for nocturnal frogs. Tiny **red-eyed tree frogs** can rest inside the leaves safe from predators.

In among the trees are thousands of tank bromeliads. They provide a watery home for small animals, and a drinking fountain for larger ones.

Pineapples are bromeliads, but they do not have tanks. The spiky leaves are the beginnings of a new plant.

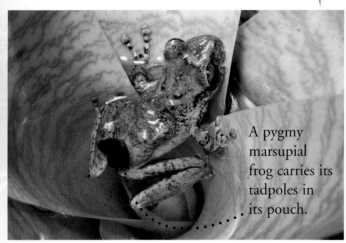

A pygmy marsupial frog carries its tadpoles in its pouch.

Birthing pool

Tadpoles need to live in water, so most frogs lay their eggs in bromeliad pools, but some lay on the forest floor. After hatching, the mother gives the tadpoles a piggyback ride up to the water.

Bromeliad leaves are stiff and strong, easily taking the weight of a passing **lizard** that has come to drink the water. The nutrients in the water also feed the plant.

Some species of tank bromeliads can hold 12 gallons (45 liters) of water!

The plant's leaves grow in a spiral, with the flowers in the middle. Most only flower once, then die.

Rain-forest clouds turn the setting sun's rays into a haze.

The sun sets quickly in the rain forest. There is little time for dusky half-light; as the sun dips behind the canopy, the forest falls dark. It also fills with the sound of frogs, bats, and insects as sunset brings them out for the night.

The **jaguar** wakes up for the night. After a quick wash, it begins to prowl for food on the ground. It is also an expert tree-climber and swimmer.

Capuchins are getting ready for bed. They search the trees, partly foraging for supper, and partly to find a safe bed for the night.

Scarlet macaws are active again now that the rain has dried up. They mate for life and are often seen flying around the forest in pairs.

The **blue morpho** smells the air with its antennae, searching for more food. It will check out new fruit by landing on it and tasting it through its legs.

The **heliconia** has yet another visitor. This time, an ant has been attracted to the sweet nectar and crawls inside the flower for a drink.

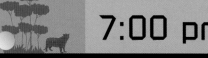
Sunset has brought a shift change for the frogs of the rain forest. Diurnal frogs, including the poison-dart frogs, go to sleep at dusk. By 7 pm, the nocturnal tree and leaf frogs are noisily patrolling the canopy, their huge eyes able to see prey—and predators—in the dark.

Poison-dart frogs disappeared at dusk…

Bright colors warn that an animal is poisonous. A **golden** poison-dart frog is extremely toxic.

Poison-dart frogs, like the **blue**, release toxins through their skin when threatened.

A single frog, such as this **green-and-black**, has enough poison to make 50 poison darts.

Strawberry poison-dart frogs are among the smallest frogs of all: just 1 in (2 cm) long.

Heliconias make great lookout posts. Look out, katydid, it's after you! for bug-spotting.

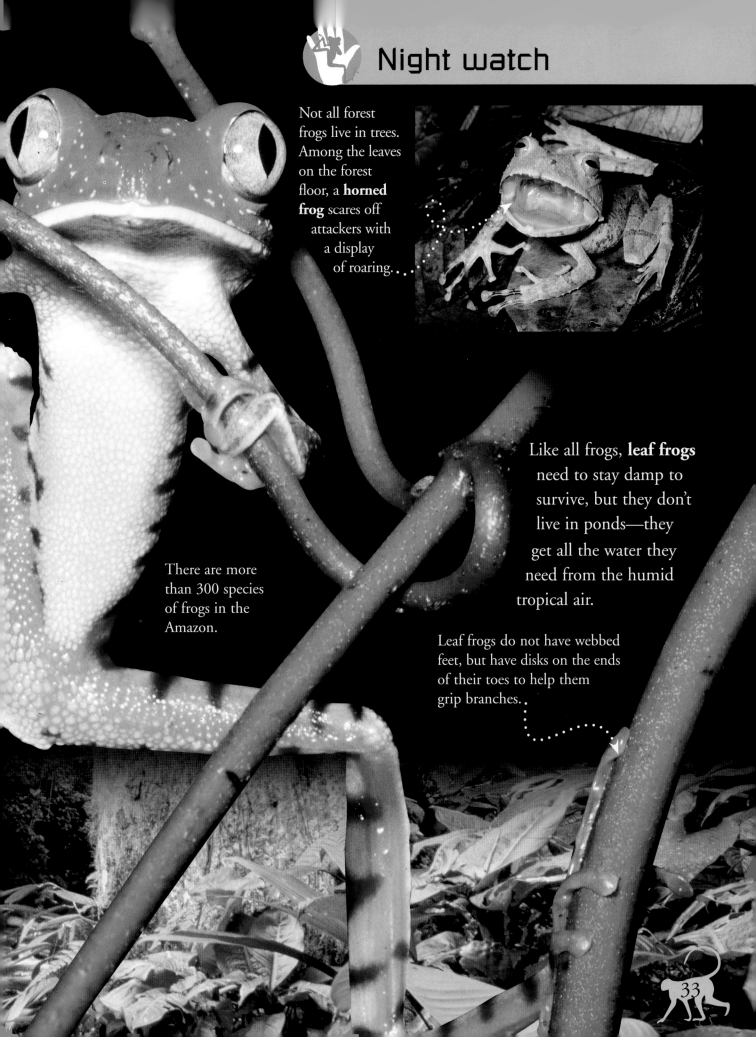

Not all forest frogs live in trees. Among the leaves on the forest floor, a **horned frog** scares off attackers with a display of roaring.

Like all frogs, **leaf frogs** need to stay damp to survive, but they don't live in ponds—they get all the water they need from the humid tropical air.

There are more than 300 species of frogs in the Amazon.

Leaf frogs do not have webbed feet, but have disks on the ends of their toes to help them grip branches.

33

Listen carefully and among the nighttime noises of the forest are lots of high-pitched clicks: the bats are out. Insect-eating bats appear first; they have been flying around since dusk. Fruit-eaters come out last.

Vampire bat

Vampire bats really do drink blood, but their saliva contains anesthetic so the bite can hardly be felt.

Fringe-lipped bats and other frog-eaters can hear the difference between poisonous and safe frogs by their calls.

Hairy-nosed bats are just one species of insect eater. Imagine tracking a tiny, moving insect only using echoes!

Rather than using sound, **fruit bats** search for food by sight and smell. Pale fruit shows up well at night.

Some bats have such large ears.

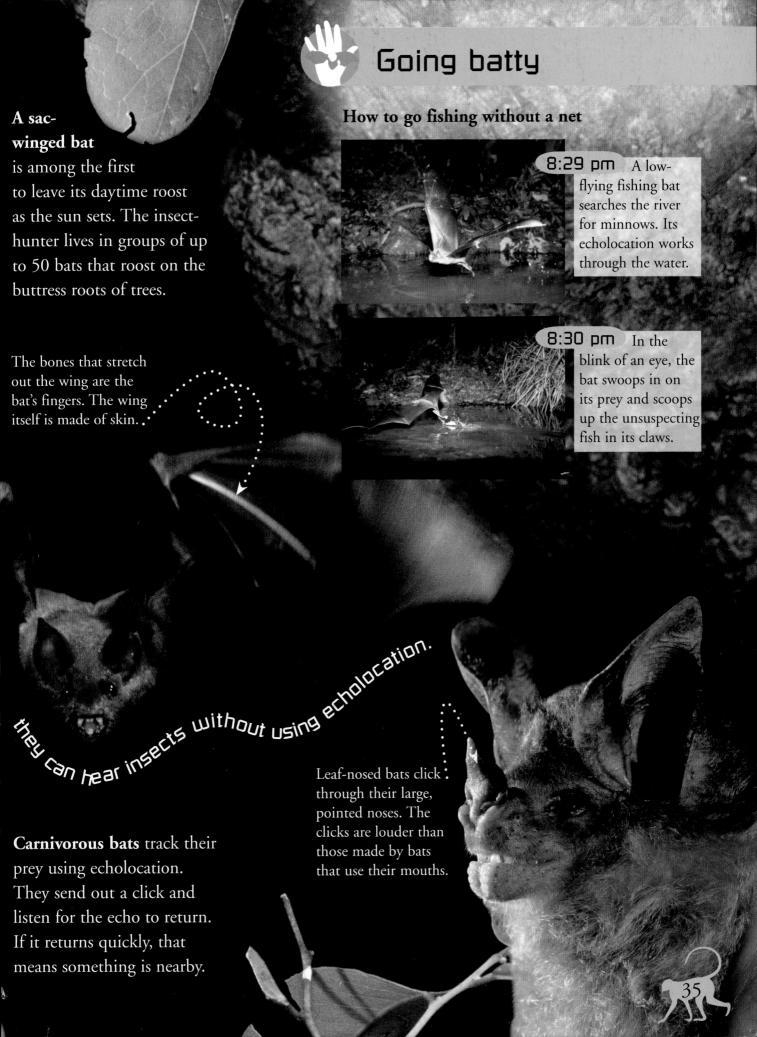

A sac-winged bat is among the first to leave its daytime roost as the sun sets. The insect-hunter lives in groups of up to 50 bats that roost on the buttress roots of trees.

The bones that stretch out the wing are the bat's fingers. The wing itself is made of skin.

they can hear insects without using echolocation.

Carnivorous bats track their prey using echolocation. They send out a click and listen for the echo to return. If it returns quickly, that means something is nearby.

How to go fishing without a net

8:29 pm A low-flying fishing bat searches the river for minnows. Its echolocation works through the water.

8:30 pm In the blink of an eye, the bat swoops in on its prey and scoops up the unsuspecting fish in its claws.

Leaf-nosed bats click through their large, pointed noses. The clicks are louder than those made by bats that use their mouths.

35

Sloths sleep for 15 hours a day, yet they are barely more active when awake. They move most at night, when they are less visible to predators.

A baby sloth hitches a ride on its mother's stomach until it is strong enough to hang from branches. ......

Going green
Algae grows in the sloth's long fur, especially in the rainy season. It provides useful camouflage for the slow-moving animal.

Sloths eat only leaves, which don't provide much energy.

Just hanging around
With their long legs and hooked claws, sloths are built for life in the trees. Their front legs are so long that they cannot walk properly on the ground.

Sloths look like they are grinning all the time. To save energy, they don't ever change their expression.

Coming down to earth

9:10 pm About every eight days, the sloth inches down the tree to the ground to go to the bathroom.

9:30 pm Once on the ground, the sloth defecates at the base of the tree. The dung is good fertilizer for the tree.

9:35 pm Sloth moths live in the sloth's fur, leaving it only to lay their eggs and feed on the dung.

1 Paca   2 Common lancehead snake

A startled paca stops in its tracks as it spots a camouflaged snake while out foraging. The highly poisonous common lancehead detects prey through the heat the animal gives out, and strikes with extreme speed.

The **jaguar** is well into its hunting. It is not a picky eater and does not search out particular prey, but will eat anything it comes across.

Capuchins sleep in small groups in tall trees. They pick a tree that is near a fruit tree, so they do not have to travel far for breakfast in the morning.

Before going to sleep, **scarlet macaws** inspect their nests. Tonight they have spotted signs of a predator and, one by one, the flock flees.

Blue morphos spend their nights hanging from the underside of leaves. They sleep in groups, returning to the same place every night.

Stiff **heliconia** stems are perfect for snakes to wrap around, poised to strike at prey. The big, strong plants are also ideal for frogs to hide in.

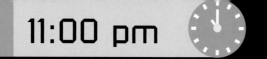
There are two types of spiders: those that spin webs, and those that hunt down prey. Both thrive in the night-time Amazon.

Brazilian huntsman spiders are the most poisonous in the world. They have enough poison to kill 225 mice—in one bite!

Tarantulas live in burrows, emerging at night to hunt insects. Their massive fangs bite down on prey, injecting poison into the victim.

Dinner is always a social occasion.

Most spiders live alone, even killing and eating each other. Not so **social spiders**. They build massive, shared webs. Working together, they can catch prey that is more than 10 times bigger than they are.

A single web can contain hundreds of social spiders.

Dinner's ready, hop to it!

Before A **jumping spider** can leap 50 times the length of its body. This one spots its prey on a nearby leaf and makes a short hop…

After …to land right on top of the unsuspecting bug. It quickly kills its prey and digs in to dinner.

Some orb weavers await prey sitting in the middle of their webs; others sit at the edge.

An orb weaver spins its round, sticky web in an open space between trees. It's a perfect place for careless insects to fly into the trap.

Under cover of darkness, small mammals go about their business of finding food while trying to avoid predators. It is not easy to see in the dark forest, so many rely on their sensitive whiskers to feel their way.

Kinkajous live entirely in the trees, surviving mostly on fruit. Sometimes called "night walkers" because they are seen at night, they are also heard chattering, calling, and making "kissing" sounds when happy.

Kinkajous have good night vision. The lining in the back of their eyes reflects light, making them glow in the dark.

Kinkajous bite straight to the nectar, which they lap up with their incredible 5-in- (13-cm-) long tongues. That's like a human child having a tongue 9 in (23 cm) long!

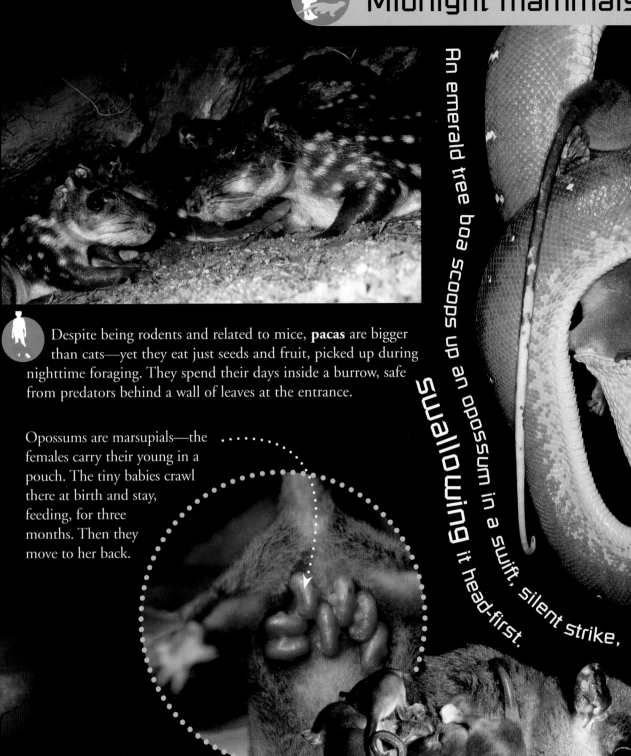

An emerald tree boa scoops up an opossum in a swift, silent strike, **swallowing** it head-first.

Despite being rodents and related to mice, **pacas** are bigger than cats—yet they eat just seeds and fruit, picked up during nighttime foraging. They spend their days inside a burrow, safe from predators behind a wall of leaves at the entrance.

Opossums are marsupials—the females carry their young in a pouch. The tiny babies crawl there at birth and stay, feeding, for three months. Then they move to her back.

A carnivorous **mouse opossum** emerges from her underground burrow to go hunting with the family. In 10 days, the babies will grow too heavy and fall off, able to hunt for themselves.

It's been a long night

of hunting for the jaguar. Finally, it catches an armadillo, killing it with one bite to the head.

The jaguar's name comes from the Mayan word *yaguar*, which means "he who kills in one leap."

Jaguar cubs live with their mother until they are two years old. In that time, she teaches them hunting skills. Even brotherly, playful wrestling is useful practice in fighting prey.

 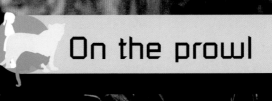

Cat cousins

Jaguars are not the only nocturnal cats. Their smaller relatives, ocelots and margays, are busy hunting prey such as frogs, insects, and monkeys.

Killer instinct

The Americas' largest cat has a fearsome bite—the second-strongest of any mammal. An armadillo's plates are no problem for its jaws.

Margays are small, arboreal cats that move around the trees much like monkeys, leaping between branches and gripping them with their paws.

Ocelots have excellent night vision, hearing, and sense of smell, which they use for tracking prey from the ground, trees, or rivers.

From dawn to dusk

Macaw

Woolly monkey

Howler monkey

Tanager

Iguana

Capuchin monkey

Heliconia

Jaguar

Agouti

Glossary

Here are the meanings of some of the important words you will come across as you read about the animals and plants of the rain forest.

ALGAE Simple plants that grow in damp places, including the fur on a sloth.

ARBOREAL Animals that are arboreal live entirely in the trees.

BRACT A leaf that grows around a plant's flower.

BRUSH A layer of shrubs and plants that cover the ground.

BUTTRESS ROOTS Large tree roots that grow above the ground because the soil is too shallow to support the tree.

CAMOUFLAGE The color or pattern of any living thing that blends in with the background,

CANOPY The tree-top layer of the rain forest. Also the branches and leaves of a single tree.

CARNIVOROUS Animals that eat meat are carnivorous.

CLAY LICK A clay-rich area, such as a riverbank, where animals go to eat clay.

DIURNAL Animals that are diurnal are active during the daytime.

ECHOLOCATION Using echoes to tell where objects are. Bats, which hunt in the dark, send out clicks and listen to the echoes to locate insects.

EMERGENT A tall tree that grows

FORAGING Grazing for food, particularly plants.

FOREST FLOOR The ground layer of the forest.

MARSUPIAL A family of mammals whose females carry their young in pouches, such as opossums.

MIGRATION The movement of animals from one place to another as the seasons change.

NOCTURNAL Animals that are nocturnal are active during the night time.

POLLINATION The process of moving pollen from one flower

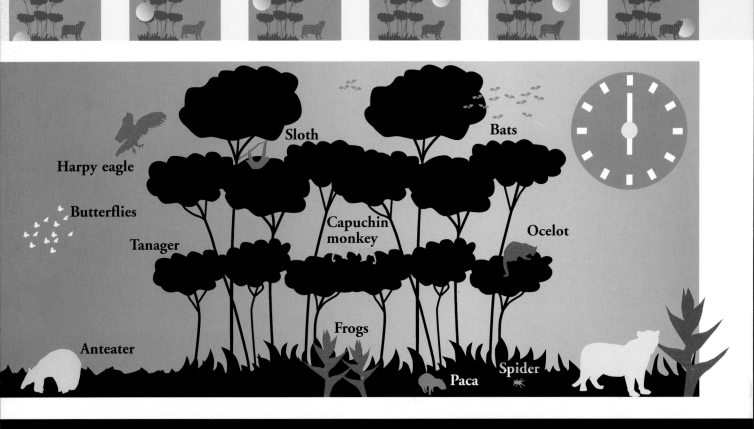

Harpy eagle

Butterflies

Tanager

Sloth

Bats

Capuchin monkey

Ocelot

Frogs

Anteater

Paca

Spider

PREDATOR An animal that hunts, kills, and eats other animals.

PREY The animal that is hunted, killed, and eaten by a predator.

PROBOSCIS A tubelike mouthpart that some insects have to suck up food.

RODENT A family of mammals that have strong teeth for chewing, such as pacas and mice.

TALON The claw of a bird of prey, such as a harpy eagle.

TROPICAL Anything that comes from the tropics, the hot zones of the world that are north and south of the equator.

UNDERSTORY The layer of the rain forest between the floor and the canopy.

Picture credits

Index